Grade 3 Flute

All Of Me John Legend 8
(Stephens/Gad)
Kobalt Music Publishing Limited/BMG Rights Management (UK) Limited.

Dancing Queen Abba 9
(Andersson/Anderson/Ulvaeus)
BOCU Music Ltd./BOCU (ABBA) Music.

Downtown Petula Clark 10
(Tony Hatch)
Sony/ATV Music Publishing (UK) Limited.

The First Cut Is The Deepest
Cat Stevens 11
(Stevens)
BMG Rights Management (UK) Limited.

Hey Jude The Beatles 12
(Lennon/McCartney)
Sony/ATV Music Publishing (UK) Limited.

Jar Of Hearts Christina Perri 13
(Perri/Lawrence/Yeretsian)
Fintage Publishing B.V./Warner/Chappell North America Limited/
BMG Rights Management (UK) Limited (Primary Wave).

Just The Way You Are Bruno Mars 14
(Levine/Hernandez/Lawrence/Cain/Walton)
Bug Music Limited/Warner/Chappell North America Limited/
Universal/MCA Music Limited/Bug Music (Windswept Account).

Let It Be The Beatles 15
(Lennon/McCartney)
Sony/ATV Music Publishing (UK) Limited.

Panic Cord Gabrielle Aplin 16
(Ashurst/Aplin/Atkinson)
Universal Music Publishing Limited/BMG Rights Management (UK) Limited/
Stage Three Music Publishing Limited.

Right Place Right Time Olly Murs 17
(Robson/Kelly/Murs)
Universal Music Publishing Limited/Imagem Music/Warner/Chappell North America Limited.

Roar Katy Perry 18
(Martin/Gottwald/McKee/Perry/Walter)
Kobalt Music Publishing Limited/BMG Rights Management (UK) Limited/
Warner/Chappell North America Limited.

Skyfall from *Skyfall* 19
(Epworth/Adkins)
Universal Music Publishing Limited/EMI Music Publishing Limited.

Someone Like You Adele 20
(Wilson/Adkins)
Chrysalis Music Limited/Universal Music Publishing Limited.

Thinking Out Loud Ed Sheeran 21
(Sheeran/Wadge)
Sony/ATV Music Publishing (UK) Limited/BDi Music Limited.

Titanium David Guetta 22
(Furler/Guetta/Tuinfort/van de Wall)
EMI Music Publishing Limited/BMG Rights Management (UK) Limited/
What A Publishing Limited.

Chester Music
part of The Music Sales Group
London/New York/Paris/Sydney/Copenhagen/Berlin/Madrid/Hong Kong/Tokyo

Published by

Chester Music
part of The Music Sales Group
14-15 Berners Street, London W1T 3LJ, UK.

Exclusive Distributors:
Music Sales Limited
Distribution Centre, Newmarket Road,
Bury St Edmunds, Suffolk IP33 3YB, UK.

Music Sales Pty Limited
Level 4, Lisgar House,
30-32 Carrington Street,
Sydney, NSW 2000 Australia.

Order No. CH84161
ISBN 978-1-78558-073-4
This book © Copyright 2015 Chester Music Limited.
All Rights Reserved.

Unauthorised reproduction of any part of this
publication by any means including photocopying
is an infringement of copyright.

Edited by Jenni Norey.
Arranged and engraved by Christopher Hussey.
With thanks to Charlotte Munro.

Printed in the EU.

Your Guarantee of Quality
As publishers, we strive to produce every book to the
highest commercial standards.
This book has been carefully designed to minimise awkward
page turns and to make playing from it a real pleasure.
Particular care has been given to specifying acid-free, neutral-sized paper
made from pulps which have not been elemental chlorine bleached.
This pulp is from farmed sustainable forests and was
produced with special regard for the environment.
Throughout, the printing and binding have been planned to
ensure a sturdy, attractive publication which should give years of enjoyment.
If your copy fails to meet our high standards,
please inform us and we will gladly replace it.

www.musicsales.com

Flute Fingering Chart

LEFT HAND
- 1ST FINGER
- 2ND FINGER
- 3L
- 3RD FINGER

RIGHT HAND
- 1ST FINGER
- Ⓐ TRILL
- 2ND FINGER
- Ⓑ TRILL
- 3RD FINGER
- 2R
- 3R
- 4R

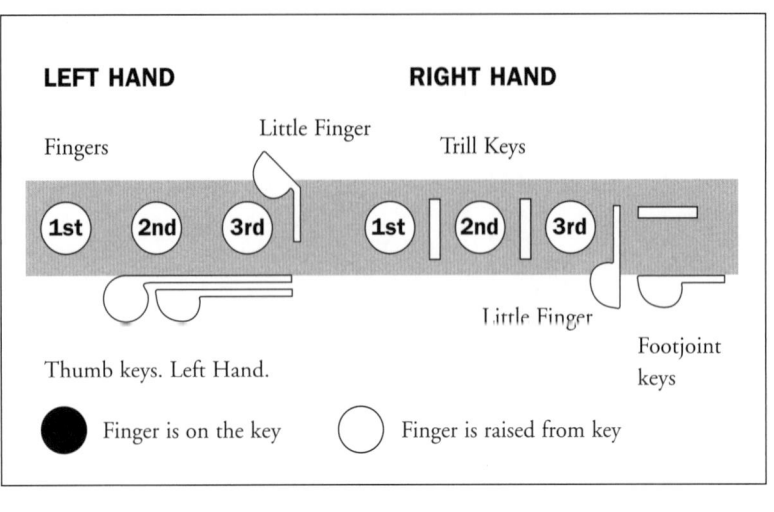

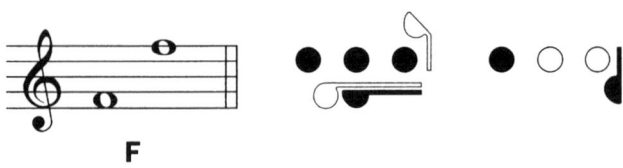

LEFT HAND
RIGHT HAND
Fingers
Little Finger
Trill Keys
1st
2nd
3rd
1st
2nd
3rd
Little Finger
Footjoint keys
Thumb keys. Left Hand.
Finger is on the key
Finger is raised from key

LEFT HAND
RIGHT HAND
C
C♯/D♭
D
D♯/E♭
E
Same fingering for both notes
F
Same fingering for both notes

LEFT HAND
RIGHT HAND
F♯/G♭
Same fingering for both notes
G
Same fingering for both notes
G♯/A♭
Same fingering for both notes
A
Same fingering for both notes
A♯/B♭
Same fingering for both notes
B
Same fingering for both notes
C
Same fingering for both notes
C♯/D♭
Same fingering for both notes

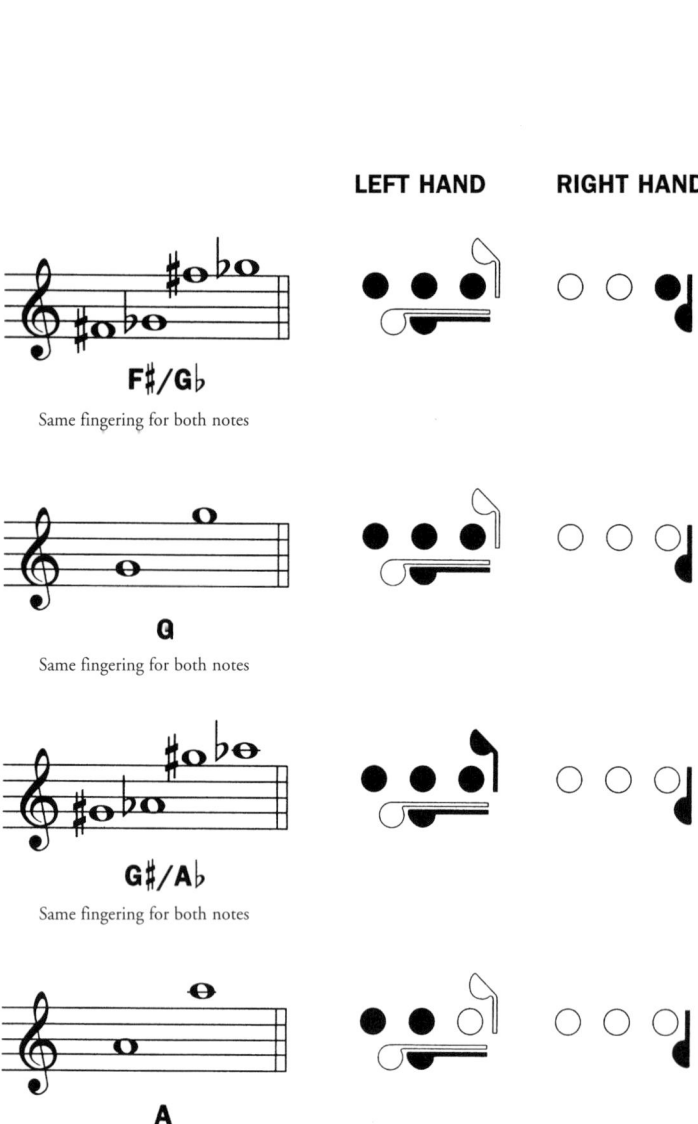

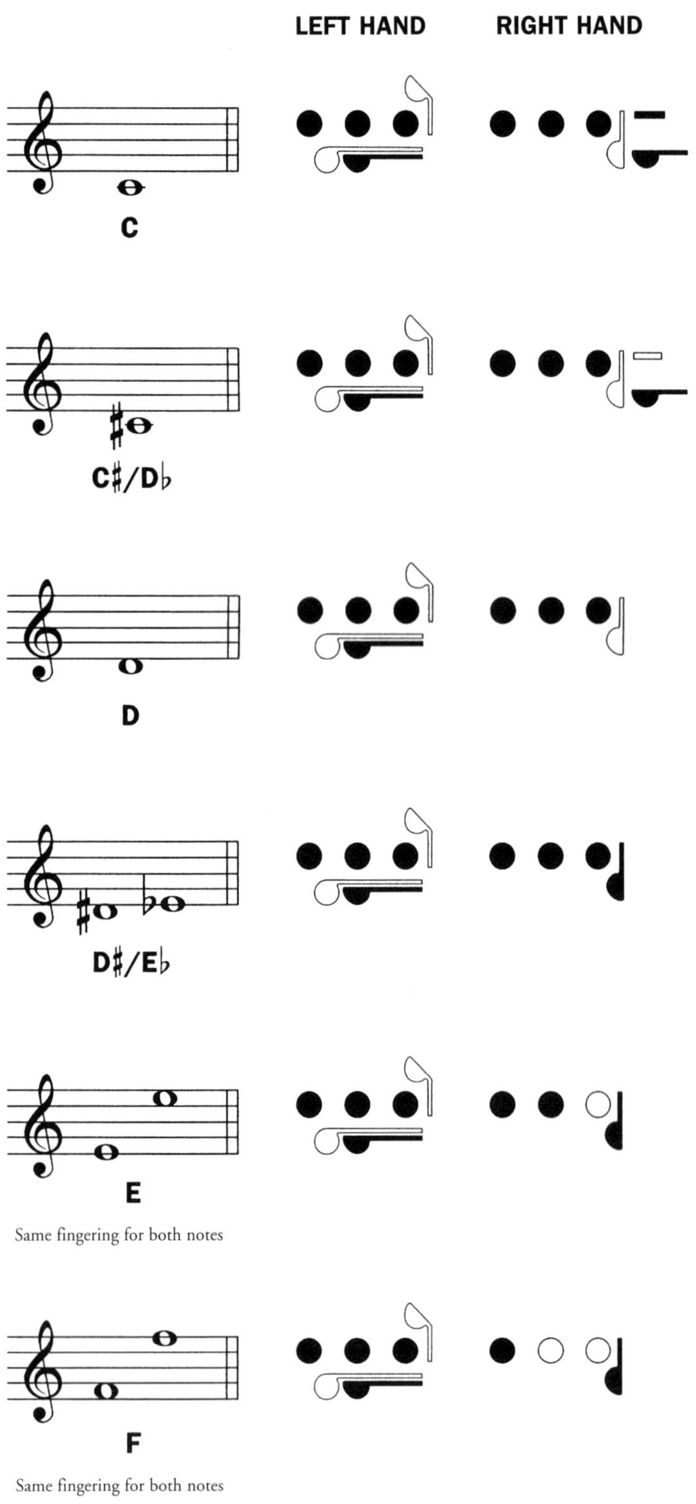

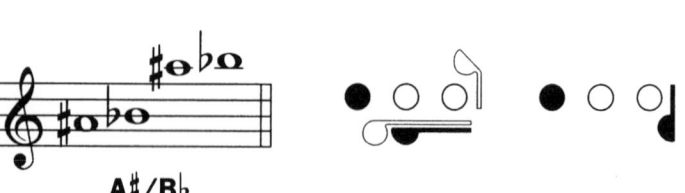

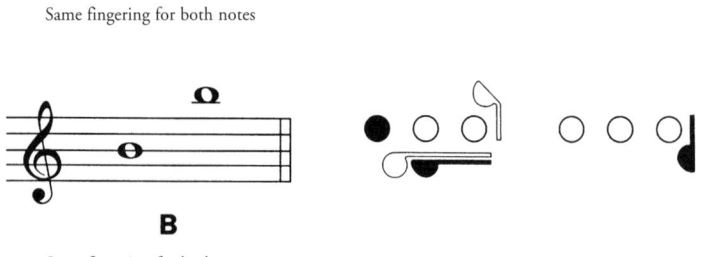

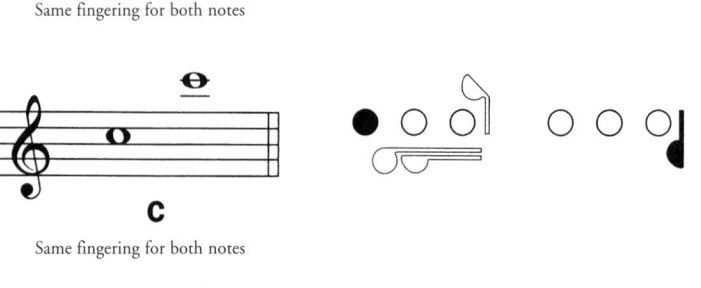

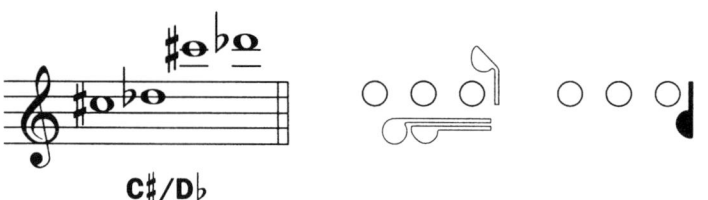

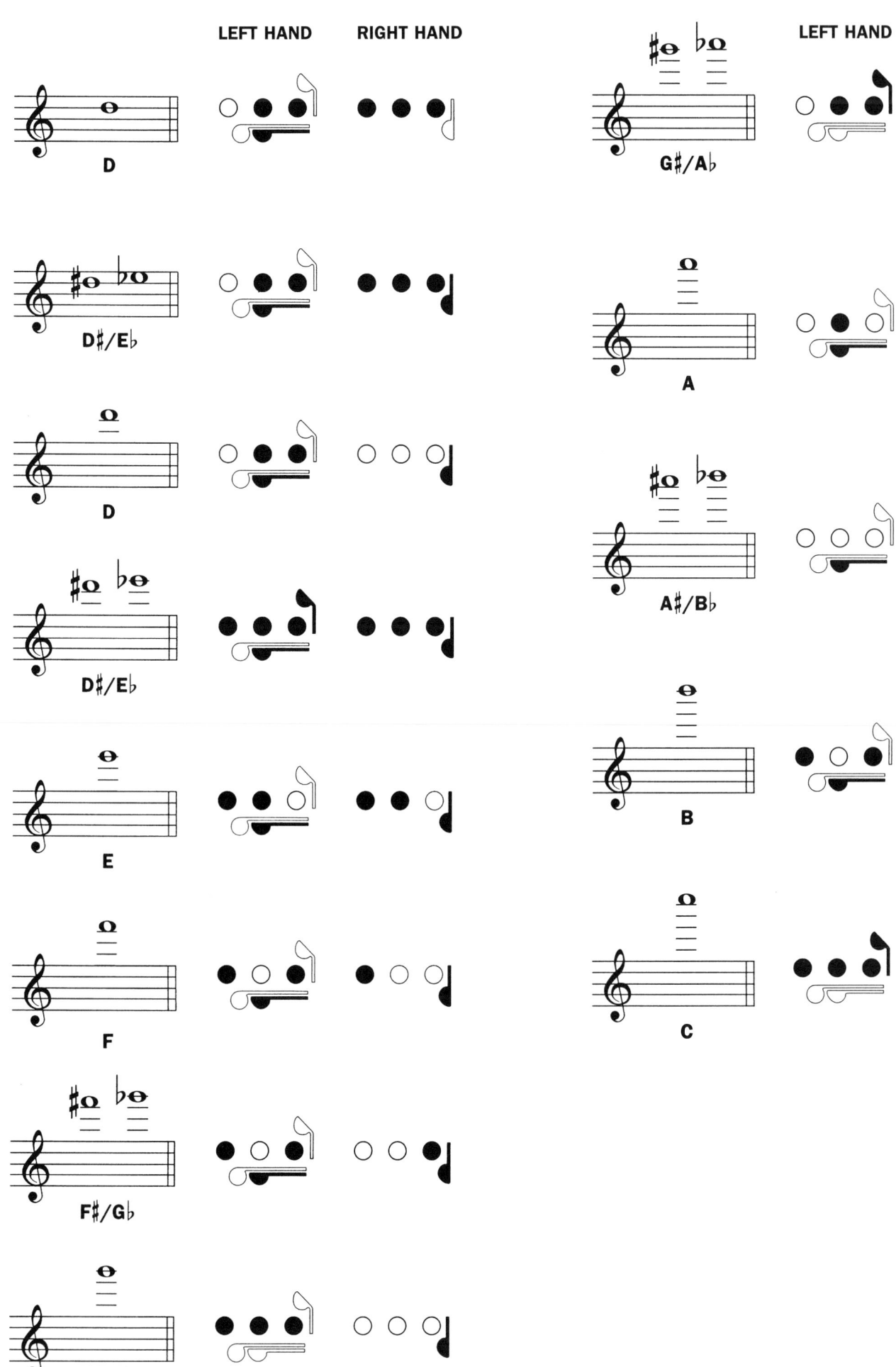

All Of Me
John Legend

This simple but effective piano and vocal based song hit the No. 1 spot in several countries, including the US, Australia, Ireland and Canada. It was written for John Legend's then-fiancé Chrissy Teigen, who he married in 2013. The video shows clips from the couple's honeymoon.

Dancing Queen
ABBA

The ultimate disco song that finally made ABBA big in the United States was originally called 'Boogaloo'. It was No. 1 Stateside and almost everywhere else in 1976. The drum part was inspired by George McCrae's 1974 disco hit 'Rock Your Baby'.

Downtown
Petula Clark

British singer Petula Clark is best known for her upbeat popular international hits of the 1960s. Released in four different languages in late 1964, 'Downtown' was a huge success in the UK, France (in both English and French versions), Netherlands, Germany, Australia, Italy, and even Rhodesia and India.

The First Cut Is The Deepest
Cat Stevens

Written by Cat Stevens in 1965, the first person to release this song was P.P. Arnold in May 1967. Stevens's own version appeared on his second album *New Masters* later the same year, and the song went on to be covered by many different artists, most notably Rod Stewart and Sheryl Crow.

Hey Jude
The Beatles

Paul was inspired to pen this lyric to console John Lennon's son, Julian, but eventually decided to change the name. At the time it was the longest 45rpm single ever released, clocking in at seven minutes 11 seconds!

Jar Of Hearts
Christina Perri

This bittersweet song about a serial heartbreaker that Christina Perri once dated became a hit in the US after it was featured on the TV show *So You Think You Can Dance?* and then on *Glee*. It spent 22 weeks in the UK charts, peaking at No. 4, and in November 2011 she performed it on the BBC's *Strictly Come Dancing* results show.

Just The Way You Are
Bruno Mars

Launching Bruno Mars into the pop stratosphere, 'Just the Way You Are' was the soulful singer-songwriter's debut single, released to worldwide acclaim in 2010. Inspired by Joe Cocker's 'You Are So Beautiful' and 'Wonderful Tonight' by Eric Clapton, the track is among the best-selling singles of all time, having sold 12.5 million copies.

Let It Be
The Beatles

The last Beatles single to be released, 'Let It Be' was issued on 6 March 1970. It is one of a few Beatles songs that exist in more than one authorised version. It was thought to be a plea for the Beatles to make their peace with each other as they started their solo careers.

Panic Cord
Gabrielle Aplin

British singer-songwriter Gabrielle Aplin first entered the charts with her piano-led cover of Frankie Goes To Hollywood's 'The Power Of Love', which was featured in the 2012 John Lewis Christmas TV advert. 'Panic Cord' is taken from her top 10 debut album *English Rain*.

Right Place Right Time
Olly Murs

'Right Place Right Time' is the title track to Olly Murs' third album. Featuring breakbeats and a prodding, rhythmic piano line that may be more familiar with electronic dance listeners, the song once again breathed fresh ideas into Murs' sound. Bursting with euphoric energy, the track was chosen as the penultimate song for the *Right Place Right Time* tour set list.

Roar
Katy Perry

As the lead single from Katy Perry's fourth studio album, *Prism*, 'Roar' was a huge international hit for the star, topping the charts in 14 countries including the UK, Australia, Canada, Ireland and New Zealand. Based on the idea of self-empowerment and standing up for yourself, the song's video features Perry playing the role of a plane crash survivor in the jungle who learns to conquer her environment by finding her inner tiger.

Skyfall
from *Skyfall*

Skyfall is the third Bond film to star Daniel Craig and the 23rd in the 007 franchise. It is one of only six films to feature the iconic Aston Martin DB5. Sung by Adele, who co-wrote the theme with Paul Epworth, this song is a strong power ballad comparable to the old Bond themes sung by Shirley Bassey.

Someone Like You
Adele

Adele's breathtaking performance of this song at the 2011 BRIT Awards led to it becoming her first No. 1 single in the UK, a position it held for five weeks. It tells the story of Adele learning of her ex-boyfriend's engagement and wishing him happiness whilst still longing to find 'someone like him'.

Thinking Out Loud
Ed Sheeran

Ed Sheeran famously wrote 'Thinking Out Loud' using a guitar gifted to him by Harry Styles of One Direction, yet piano features heavily on this steady-paced ballad that celebrates the enduring quality of love and romance.

Titanium
David Guetta

Despite being offered to several vocalists, including Katy Perry, David Guetta's 'Titanium' was finally released with the artist who co-wrote the song and recorded the demo singing lead vocals: Australian singer Sia. This song proved a big hit for both of them, claiming a top 10 spot in over 15 countries.

All Of Me

Words & Music by John Stephens and Toby Gad

© Copyright 2013 John Legend Publishing and Gad Songs, LLC. All Rights for John Legend Publishing Administered by BMG Rights Management (US) LLC.
All Rights for Gad Songs, LLC Administered by Atlas Music Group.

Carefully observe the dynamics in this song.

The melody is quite high from bar 29, going up to a top G, so make sure you have taken a good breath so you can control the top notes.

Dancing Queen

Words & Music by Benny Andersson, Stig Anderson & Björn Ulvaeus

© Copyright 1976 Universal/Union Songs Musikforlag AB. Bocu Music Limited for Great Britain and the Republic of Ireland.
Universal Music Publishing Limited for World excluding Great Britain and the Republic of Ireland. All Rights Reserved. International Copyright Secured.

This song requires plenty of drive and energy! The time signature is ¢ (known as *cut common time*), which shows us there are two minim beats per bar—this can also be written as $\frac{2}{2}$.

Downtown

Words & Music by Tony Hatch

© Copyright 1964 Sony/ATV Music Publishing.
All Rights Reserved. International Copyright Secured.

Keep the quavers bouncy and light in this song to create a cheerful feel.

Don't forget to start the crescendo at bar 19 very softly so you can build gradually all the way to *forte* (*f*) at bar 22.

The First Cut Is The Deepest

Words & Music by Cat Stevens

© Copyright 1967 Salafa Limited. BMG Rights Management (UK) Limited.
All Rights Reserved. International Copyright Secured.

The marking *cantabile* tells you to play 'in a singing style', so aim for a lovely singing tone quality.
Remember to raise your left-hand first finger for the many E♭s in this song.

Hey Jude

Words & Music by John Lennon & Paul McCartney

© Copyright 1968 Sony/ATV Music Publishing.
All Rights Reserved. International Copyright Secured.

Practise the rhythm in bars 11 and 16 on its own, and without slurs and ties, until you are confident. Watch out for the 2/4 bar (bar 21) and play the *coda* with a good strong sound.

Jar Of Hearts

Words & Music by Christina Perri, Drew Lawrence & Barrett Yeretsian

© Copyright 2010 WB Music Corp/Miss Perri Lane Publishing/Primary Wave Yeretsian/Piggy Dog Music.
Copyright Control/Fintage Publishing. B.V./Warner/Chappell North America Limited /BMG Rights Management (UK) Limited (Primary Wave).
All Rights Reserved. International Copyright Secured.

Aim for a gentle sound when you start this bittersweet song. The notes are quite low so take care not to force the sound.

Just The Way You Are

Words & Music by Ari Levine, Bruno Mars, Philip Lawrence, Khari Cain & Khalil Walton

© Copyright 2010 Universal Music Corporation, USA/WB Music Corporation/Art For Art's Sake Music/Toy Plane Music/Upper Dec, USA/Roc Nation Music, USA/
Music Famamanem, USA/Mars Force Music, USA/Northside Independent Music Publishing, USA/Music Of Windswept.
Bug Music Limited/Warner/Chappell North America Limited/Universal/MCA Music Limited/Bug Music (Windswept Account).
All Rights Reserved. International Copyright Secured.

Perfect the rhythm in bars 8–12 before moving on.

Take deep breaths to help produce a good *forte* (***f***) from bar 25 onwards, but take care not to blow too high so the pitch goes sharp.

Let It Be

Words & Music by John Lennon & Paul McCartney

© Copyright 1970 Sony/ATV Music Publishing.
All Rights Reserved. International Copyright Secured.

This song makes use of all three registers on the flute. If you find bars 33–41 tricky, try practising one or two bars at a time, taking care with the fingerings of top G, F and E♭.

Remember to count two minims per bar.

Panic Cord

Words & Music by Jez Ashurst, Gabrielle Aplin & Nicholas Atkinson

© Copyright 2013 Major 3rd Music Limited. Universal Music Publishing Limited/BMG Rights Management (UK) Limited/Stage Three Music Publishing Limited.
All Rights Reserved. International Copyright Secured.

This song is in the key of D major. Make sure you always replace your right-hand little finger after playing D, or the pitch of the new note may sound flat.

Right Place Right Time

Words & Music by Stephen Robson, Claude Kelly & Oliver Murs

© Copyright 2013 Studio Beast Music/Salli Isaak Music Publishing Limited/Imagem CV/Warner-Tamerlane Publishing Co.
Universal Music Publishing Limited/Imagem Music/Warner/Chappell North America Limited. All Rights Reserved. International Copyright Secured.

This song requires lots of energy, and gives you a chance to shine in the upper register of the flute.
Remember to breathe deeply so you are able to produce a strong sound at bar 23.

Roar

Words & Music by Max Martin, Lukasz Gottwald, Bonnie McKee, Katy Perry & Henry Russell Walter

© Copyright 2013 Kasz Money Publishing/When I'm Rich You'll Be My Bitch/Where Da Kasz At/Bonnie McKee Music/Prescription Songs/CYP Two Publishing/
MXM Music AB/Cirkut Breaker LLC. Downtown Music Publishing LLC/Warner/Chappell North America Limited /Kobalt Music Publishing Limited.
All Rights Reserved. International Copyright Secured.

Note the different uses of articulation in this song—*legato* to begin with, *staccato* from bar 11, returning to *legato* at bar 18 (with an *accent* just before the double bar line), and including *staccato* notes from bar 27 again. In bars 27, 28 and 29, some notes have a staccato mark and a slur to them, which tells you to 'throw them away', so they should be short and light, but not tongued.

Skyfall

Words & Music by Paul Epworth & Adele Adkins

© Copyright 2012 Melted Stone Publishing Ltd. Universal Music Publishing Limited/EMI Music Publishing Limited.
All Rights Reserved. International Copyright Secured.

Aim to create a peaceful atmosphere at the beginning of this song by keeping your sound soft and gentle. Don't forget to crescendo to the *forte* (*f*) in bar 25 to provide a strong contrast.

dim. al niente tells you to diminuendo to nothing at the end.

Someone Like You

Words & Music by Daniel Wilson & Adele Adkins

© Copyright 2010 Sugar Lake Music LLC/Melted Stone Publishing Limited. Chrysalis Music Limited, a BMG Chrysalis company/Universal Music Publishing Limited.
All Rights Reserved. International Copyright Secured.

To keep the tranquil mood of the opening section, keep your sound soft but 'singing' in quality.

The chorus, beginning in bar 22, is a chance to show off your control of the upper register of the flute.

Thinking Out Loud

Words & Music by Ed Sheeran & Amy Wadge

© Copyright 2014 Sony/ATV Music Publishing/BDi Music Limited.
All Rights Reserved. International Copyright Secured.

Try playing the repeated phrases in this song slightly differently each time to add interest—try adding your own dynamics or articulation marks.

Watch out for the quaver triplets—in bars 30, 32 and 34, the quaver rest is part of the triplet group, so you could add another A in place of the rest while you practise, and then omit it when you are confident.

Titanium

Words & Music by Sia Furler, David Guetta, Giorgio Tuinfort & Nick van de Wall

© Copyright 2011 Piano Songs/Afrojack Publishing. EMI Music Publishing Limited/BMG Rights Management (UK) Limited/What A Publishing Limited.
All Rights Reserved. International Copyright Secured.

The last section of this song is played *fortissimo* (**ff**), requiring a lot of power and drive! Make sure your top notes sound bold and strong without going sharp.

COLLECT THE SERIES
Graded Flute Pieces
15 Popular Practice Pieces

Grade 1 Flute Pieces
CH84139

Grade 2 Flute Pieces
CH84150

Grade 3 Flute Pieces
CH84161

Available from all good music shops

or, in case of difficulty contact:
Music Sales Limited, Newmarket Road, Bury St Edmunds, Suffolk, IP33 3YB, UK.
music@musicsales.co.uk

HOW TO DOWNLOAD YOUR MUSIC TRACKS

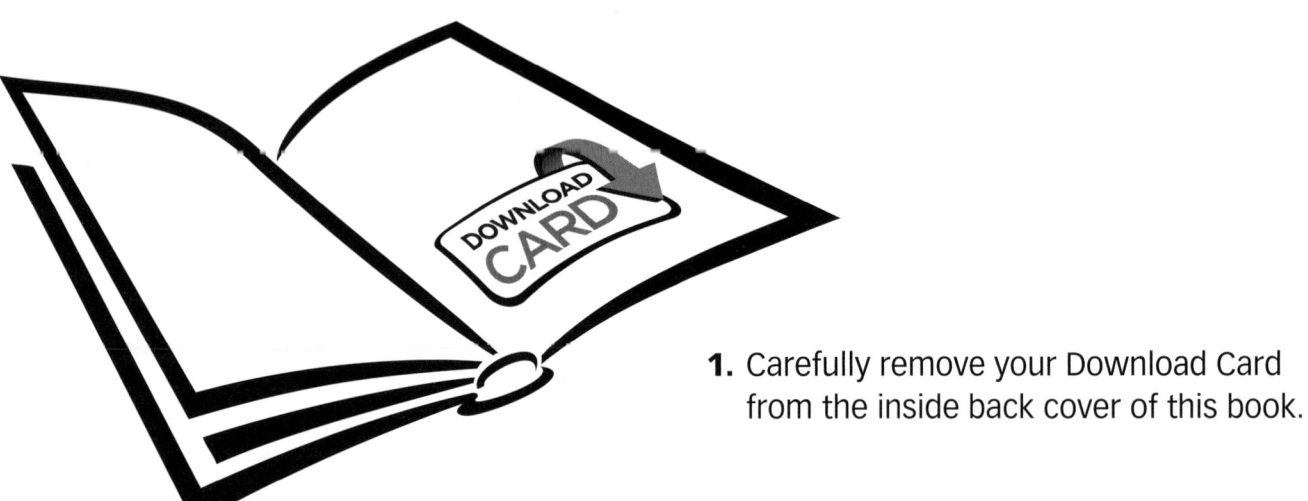

1. Carefully remove your Download Card from the inside back cover of this book.

2. On the back of the card is your unique access code. Enter this at www.musicsalesdownloads.com

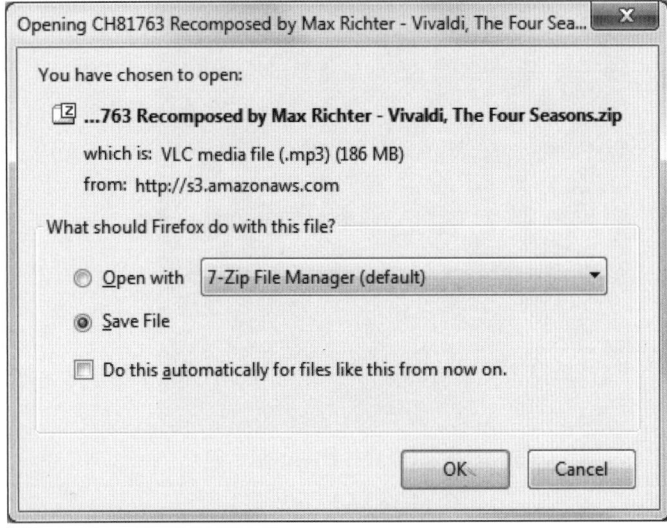

3. Follow the instructions to save your files to your computer*. That's it!

*Appearance of download manager will vary depending upon operating system and web browser.
In case of difficulty when downloading files, please contact dropcards.com/help
Card missing? Please contact music@musicsales.co.uk